USING A
COLOSTOMY BAG

BY HARRIET BRUNDLE

HUMAN BODY HELPERS

BookLife PUBLISHING

©2019
BookLife Publishing Ltd.
King's Lynn
Norfolk PE30 4LS

All rights reserved.
Printed in Malaysia.

A catalogue record for this book is available from the British Library.

ISBN: 978-1-78637-788-3

Written by:
Harriet Brundle

Edited by:
John Wood

Designed by:
Danielle Rippengill

All facts, statistics, web addresses and URLs in this book were verified as valid and accurate at time of writing. No responsibility for any changes to external websites or references can be accepted by either the author or publisher.

The author of this book is not a medically trained professional. If you have any questions about colostomy bags, please see your doctor.

IMAGE CREDITS

All images are courtesy of Shutterstock.com, unless otherwise specified. With thanks to Getty Images, Thinkstock Photo and iStockphoto. Front Cover & 1 – Beatriz Gascon J, NikaMooni, rumruay. Carlos – Beatriz Gascon J. Charlie – rumruay. 2 – Zentangle. 5 – Beatriz Gascon J. 6 – Zentangle. 7 – Beatriz Gascon J. 11 – EstherQueen999. 15 – Zentangle. 18 – EstherQueen999. 19 – WindAwake. 22 – flatvector.

CONTENTS

PAGE 4   What Is the Colon?
PAGE 6   What Is a Colostomy?
PAGE 8   What Is a Colostomy Bag?
PAGE 10 Why Might I Need a Colostomy Bag?
PAGE 12 What Happens at the Hospital?
PAGE 16 What Happens After My Operation?
PAGE 18 How Do I Change My Colostomy Bag?
PAGE 20 Dos and Don'ts
PAGE 22 Life After Your Colostomy Bag
PAGE 24 Glossary and Index

Words that look like **this** can be found in the glossary on page 24.

WHAT IS THE COLON?

Your intestines are a long tube which connect your stomach to your anus.

Your intestines have two parts: the small intestine and the large intestine. The large intestine is also known as your colon.

Hi! I'm Carlos and I'm your colon.

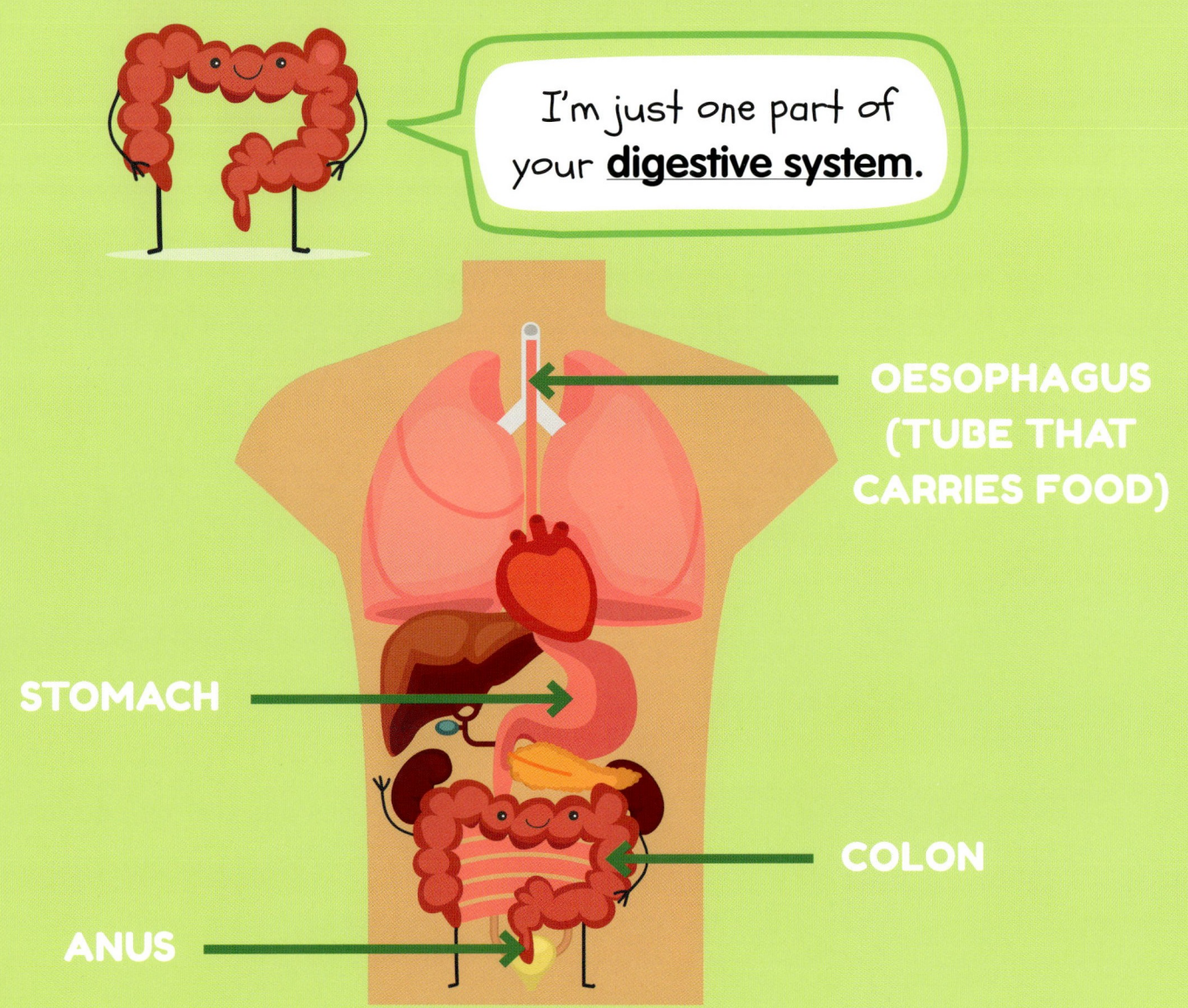

Inside your colon, any waste that your body doesn't need is formed into poo, also called stool. When you go to the toilet, your body is getting rid of the waste.

WHAT IS A COLOSTOMY?

A colostomy is an **operation** where a healthy part of your colon is cut and pulled through an opening made in your tummy. The operation is done at the hospital.

Don't worry! You won't feel anything during the operation.

The opening made in your tummy is called a stoma. After the operation, the waste you would usually pass from your anus now comes out of your stoma.

WHAT IS A COLOSTOMY BAG?

Hi, I'm Charlie and I'm a colostomy bag.

A colostomy bag is a small bag which attaches to your stoma. The bag is used to safely collect the waste that now comes from your stoma.

Colostomy bags are waterproof so they don't leak. Many bags also have a filter, which means that other people don't notice any smell. The bag is small enough to wear under your clothes.

You can hardly notice me!

WHY MIGHT I NEED A COLOSTOMY BAG?

There are lots of different reasons why you might need a colostomy bag. You might have a problem with your colon or have an injury or illness which means you can't pass poo normally.

Ouch! This is painful!

If you feel pain or have problems when you're going to the toilet, it's important that you tell an adult. It might not be a problem at all, but it is always best to be checked by a doctor.

WHAT HAPPENS AT THE HOSPITAL?

"Hi Carlos, I'm going to be your colostomy bag. My name is Charlie."

"Hi Charlie, it's nice to meet you."

The doctor might say you need a colostomy operation at the hospital. Before you have the operation, you'll be told all about what's going to happen.

After your operation, you may need to stay in hospital for a few days. You'll be given medicine, usually through a **drip**, to make sure you're not in any pain.

It won't be long before we get to go home, Carlos.

While you're at the hospital, you will be shown how to take care of your stoma. It's really important that you keep the opening clean so that the skin doesn't become **infected**.

Please don't forget to look after me!

A special nurse called a stoma nurse will show you how to empty and change your colostomy bag. If you have any questions, your stoma nurse will be able to help.

Don't worry if you can't do it first time. It might take some practice.

WHAT HAPPENS AFTER MY OPERATION?

After you have had your operation, you might find that your colostomy bag takes a little bit of getting used to. You might feel some pain at first or feel very aware of your bag.

You'll soon get used to me, Carlos!

The doctors will tell you the foods you should and shouldn't be eating.

You may need to change what kinds of food you eat after your operation while you get used to having a colostomy bag. You should be able to eat normally again after a few weeks.

HOW DO I CHANGE MY COLOSTOMY BAG?

When you need to change your colostomy bag, make sure you have everything you need to hand before you start. Wash your hands and carefully peel off the used colostomy bag.

It's really important that your hands are clean before you start.

Clean your stoma gently with warm water or a wipe, but try not to rub the area. Once the skin around your stoma is dry, you can carefully stick on your new colostomy bag.

DOS AND DON'TS

DO make sure when you leave the house that you, or an adult with you, have got everything needed to change your colostomy bag.

DON'T get any creases in the part of the bag that sticks to your body.

DO remember to clean your stoma every time you change your colostomy bag.

DON'T forget you need to change your colostomy bag as soon as it starts getting full.

LIFE AFTER YOUR COLOSTOMY BAG

In some cases, a colostomy operation can be <u>reversed</u>. This means that your colon is **<u>reattached</u>** and you can pass poo as you did before you had a colostomy bag.

Some people will need to have a colostomy bag for the rest of their lives. For most people, once they're used to using their colostomy bag it doesn't affect day-to-day life too much.

GLOSSARY

ANUS — the opening in the bottom where waste leaves the body

DIGESTIVE SYSTEM — the parts of the body that work together to break food down and produce energy

DRIP — a small tube put under the skin to give medicine straight into the body

INFECTED — something affected by a disease

OPERATION — something done on a body to remove or mend something

REATTACHED — being attached to something again

REVERSED — put back to how it was before

STOMACH — a sack-like part of the body through which food passes

INDEX

CLEAN 14, 18–19, 21
COLONS 4–6, 10, 22
DOCTORS 11–12, 17
FOOD 5, 17
HOSPITALS 6, 12–14
OPERATIONS 6–7, 12–13, 16–17, 22
PAIN 10–11, 13, 16
POO 5, 10, 22
STOMAS 6–8, 14–15, 19, 21
TUMMIES 6–7
WASTE 5, 7–8